YVETTE PIM

0118 987 4514

What people are saying about 101 Ways to Improve Your Communication Skills Instantly!

"Jo and Bennie have put together a clear, concise format for improving your communication skills. This book delivers it in delightful bite-sized chunks that are easy to read and apply. I recommend this text to anyone seeking self-improvement."
–Bernard Hale Zick, CEO
International Society of Speakers,
Authors and Consultants

"Whether a business fails or succeeds often depends more on communication skills than technical know how. This fine book helps you, the business person, improve all aspects of communicating, speaking, writing, listening, and the most important nonverbal elements: body language, behavior and attitudes, to help you win your clients, prospects, suppliers and all other associates over to you. Jo and Bennie are supremely qualified to help you make your business soar!"
–Judit Sinclair, Managing Director
Tymbrand Pty Ltd, Sidney, Australia

"A masterful, affirming, practical and creative guide to effective communication skills. This book will help you improve your everyday interaction with friends, family, and the ever-changing business environment. Years of 'know how' and 'want to' have driven the authors of this GREAT book, to share their skills with you."
–Ronald L. Lewis, Chairman, CEO
National Association of Small Businesses

D0197431

"A very useful and informative book—of high value to those who need to be really clear communicators."

–Nancy Brinker, Founder
Susan G. Komen Breast Cancer Foundation

"Great list of communication strategies! In one reading of the book I found many tips to improve my communication with family, friends, students, staff, parents and community members. Thanks for providing such a valuable tool!"

–Mary Ann Ryan, Principal
Annandale Terrace Elementary School

"A perceptive and concise compendium of ways for novices and skilled professionals to enhance their communication skills. Buy it today, use it tomorrow."

–Deborah H. Alderson
Senior Vice President, Techmatics

"Communication skills are essential for corporate survival. I not only find this book a quick reference and an easy-to-use guide for my communication challenges, but I also insist that every member of my management team read it, study it, and keep a copy of it on their desks at all times!"

–Johnny (Pawe) T. Uy
President and General Manager
Rosita's (Cebu) Inc, Philippines

101
Ways to Improve Your Communication Skills Instantly

Jo Condrill

Bennie Bough, Ph.D.

101 Ways to Improve Your Communication Skills Instantly

by Jo Condrill and
Bennie Bough, Ph.D.

Published by:
The Catalyst Group
1 Berghem Mews
Blythe Road
London
W14 0HN

All rights reserved. No part of this book may be reproduced or transmitted in any form or by any means, electronic or mechanical, including photocopying or recording or by any information storage or retrieval system, without permission in writing from the publisher or authors.

Copyright © 1998 by Jo Condrill and
Bennie Bough, Ph.D.

Printed in Great Britain by
Redwood Books, Trowbridge, Wiltshire

Library of Congress Catalog Card Number: 97-97110

Condrill, Jo and Bough, Bennie, Ph.D.
    101 Ways to Improve Your Communication Skills Instantly /
by Jo Condrill and Bennie Bough, Ph.D.

ISBN 0-9661414-7-4
            1. Reference   2. Business   3. Communication

Book and Cover Design by Joe Arunski and Barbara Lehman
Illustrations by Steve Ferchaud

Contents

PART I - COMMUNICATION

Know What You Want to Say - Control Fear - Stop Talking and Listen - Think Before You Talk - Believe in Your Message - Repeat Major Points - Find Out What Your Listener Wants

Define Acronyms - Reduce Jargon - Level Objections - Use Humor - Use Anecdotes and Stories - Ask for Feedback - Increase Your Vocabulary - Eliminate Audible Pauses - Enunciate Clearly - Practice Pronouncing Words Properly - Exercise Tongue, Jaws, and Lips - Make Eye Contact - Gesture - Pause - Speak More Slowly - Speak Faster - Vary Your Volume - Watch Your Tone - Record Your Voice

Prepare to Listen - Focus on the Speaker - Screen Out Distractions - Concentrate on the Message - Listen to Tapes While You Commute

Ask Questions - Avoid Daydreaming - Accept Accents - Use Mind-Mapping - Interview - Complaints - Telephone - Attend a Toastmasters Meeting

PART II - SPEAKING AND WRITING

PART III - GENERAL TIPS

Dedication

*To our families and friends who listened
patiently, critiqued kindly, and lovingly
encouraged us in this endeavor.
To you, the reader, that you may be inspired
to act on the information you find here.*

INTRODUCTION

Have you ever embarrassed yourself by making a grammatical error in an important interview or conversation? Have you mispronounced a word or used an incorrect term? We all have made these and other communication blunders at one time or another.

Here is a small book that's big on recommendations that you can put into action immediately to improve your communication skills. We realize that "know how" and "want to" are two essentials for success. This book provides "know how," and all you have to add is the "want to." Only you can decide to improve your communication skills.

We have tried and tested these techniques. We have seen changes in our own development. We have seen the results in others, and we know these changes can occur instantly. We don't expect you to implement all 101 ways at one time, but each time you implement one of them, you will experience success instantly. Our successes have provided the inspiration for this book. We know that if you begin to apply the methods in this book you, too, will experience success instantly. Make a commitment to continue improving over a period of time. Lifelong learning is the mark of all successful individuals.

HOW WILL YOU BENEFIT BY IMPROVING YOUR COMMUNICATION SKILLS?

• More pay and perks because of greater potential for advancement at work.

• Greater harmony and opportunity to get what you want with a reduced chance of misunderstandings.

• Greater exposure to new ideas resulting in a broader understanding of world events.

• Enhanced feelings of safety and friendship with less likelihood of hostility.

• Increased pride in personal performance and a more expansive view of possibilities.

• Increased quality of life with improved relationships.

WHO CAN BENEFIT FROM THIS BOOK?
Professionals
Parents
Students
Salespeople
Business persons
Homemakers
Ministers
Volunteers

In short, just about everyone! Can you think of anyone who couldn't benefit from improved communication skills? Neither could we! But the preceding groups will find it especially rewarding.

HOW CAN YOU, AS AN INDIVIDUAL, GAIN MAXIMUM BENEFIT FROM THIS BOOK?

Flip through it. Look at the headings and quotations. Skim the Contents page. Run your fingers over the index pages. Then:

- Go through it page by page.

- Put a check mark on those pages you are confident you have mastered.

- Go back and prioritize the others.

- Set a target date to have each one completed.

- Begin to focus on one page at a time until you understand the concept.

- Put it into practice.

- When you have mastered the skill, move on to the next.

Especially in the "behavioral" areas, you need to **decide** to change, then practice the techniques.

Start now! Set a goal to complete the book in a given time and assign yourself rewards at certain milestones. Measure your progress and then treat yourself.

May your journey of self-development be a lifelong pursuit with many pauses to celebrate your achievements!

ACKNOWLEDGMENTS

We could never have completed this book without a little help from our friends and relatives. We are very grateful for their stimulating ideas and helpful suggestions.

Kathi Bough

Resa Motsch

Kristopher Bough

Sara Bough Polen

Bess Crouch

Addie Richmond

Dilip Abayasekara, Ph.D.

Michael Wardinski, Ph.D.

Bill Bruce

Art Horn

Gwendolyn Talbot

Terry Schutt

June Cottrell-Miller

Isaac Treadwell

James Heeren

James Diamond

Larry Welch

Randyl "Blake" Mitchell

and our Master Mind partners,

Tom Grady and

Art Jackson

DISCLAIMER

This book is designed to provide information regarding the subject matter covered. It is sold with the understanding that the publisher and authors are not engaged in rendering legal, accounting or other professional services. If legal or other expert assistance is required, the services of a competent professional should be sought.

It is not the purpose of this manual to reprint all the information that is otherwise available to the authors and/or publisher, but to complement, amplify and supplement other texts. You are urged to read all the available material and learn as much as possible about communications.

Every effort has been made to make this manual as accurate as possible. However, there may be mistakes both typographical and in content. Therefore, this text should be used only as a general guide and not as the ultimate source of speaking, listening, and writing.

The purpose of this manual is to educate and entertain. The authors and publisher shall have neither liability nor responsibility to any person or entity with respect to any loss or damage caused, or alleged to be caused, directly or indirectly by the information contained in this book.

If you do not wish to be bound by the above, you may return this book to the publisher for a full refund.

KNOW WHAT YOU WANT TO SAY

By listening, thinking and formulating your thoughts before you speak, you will increase your effectiveness as a powerful communicator.

- Think before you talk.

- Know your message.

- Get to the point quickly. Then, it is easier for the listener to remember what you said.

- Know the outcome you want from your conversation.

- Practice the power of persuasion. Almost everything we say is an attempt to persuade the other person to accept our point of view.

- For successful networking, plan in advance what you want to say and what you want to accomplish.

- Know something about the people you'll be talking to.

. . . .

I think, therefore I am.
–Descartes

PART I – COMMUNICATION – SPEAKING

CONTROL FEAR

Fear is a defense mechanism to protect ourselves. We fear destruction of our self-esteem. Who we are is precious to us. Others' words about us can seem like building blocks either supporting us or crashing in on us. Fear focuses on the worst thing that can happen. "I'll fail. I'll forget what I'm going to say. I'll be humiliated. I'll panic. I'll stop breathing." Instead, shift your focus with the following tips:

• Focus on the

  -Listener, (not yourself.)

  -Message, (not the words.)

  -Success, (not the alternatives.)

• Visualize a positive outcome.

• Take a deep breath, relax, and be yourself.

• Do your homework, know what you want to say.

• Control your negative self-talk.

• Speak from the heart rather than the ego.

....

The only thing we have to fear is fear itself.
–Franklin D. Roosevelt

PART I–COMMUNICATION–SPEAKING

STOP TALKING AND LISTEN

Conversation should be like a tennis match, each person having a turn to give and receive. The true art of conversation is talking and listening.

• Allow your conversation partner to speak.

• Respect the other person's point of view.

• Concentrate on the conversation. Thinking about what **you** will say rather than actively listening will cause you to miss vital information.

• Help individuals resolve their own problems with patient listening. They have the ability to solve their own problems.

....

Dean Rusk, the former Secretary of State, said that the best way to persuade others is with our ears—by listening.

PART I-COMMUNICATION-SPEAKING

THINK BEFORE YOU TALK

If you give attention to what you will say, you increase your chances of persuading the other person to your point of view. You will also decrease the chances of making a mistake or social blunder.

• Pause, think and consider what you want to say.

• Choose appropriate words that clearly express your message.

• Decide on the tone you want in your conversation.

• Determine the outcome you want from your interchange.

• Know your audience, and if possible, their viewpoint and level of understanding about the subject matter.

• Shape your message to be easily understood.

....

Thinking is a momentary dismissal of irrelevancies.
–Richard Buckminster Fuller

PART I–COMMUNICATION–SPEAKING

BELIEVE IN YOUR MESSAGE

Believe in your message because this is the crux of any successful communication. When you passionately believe in your message, your verbal and nonverbal communications will flow freely.

• Speak with passion and conviction.

• Allow your feelings, delivery, body language and voice to flow naturally.

• Show your enthusiasm.

• Avoid faking it or you risk losing your credibility.

Never let the fear of striking out get in your way.
–George Herman ("Babe") Ruth

PART I-COMMUNICATION-SPEAKING

REPEAT MAJOR POINTS

Repetition reinforces the speaker's main points and aids in listener's retention.

• Know your major points.

• Paraphrase, as needed, in different ways throughout your conversation to reemphasize.

• Tactfully ask your listener for feedback.

• Ask questions that will indicate the listener understands your main points.

••

Repetition is the cadence of the universe.
–Claude Bristol

PART I–COMMUNICATION–SPEAKING

FIND OUT WHAT YOUR LISTENER WANTS

To gain the most from any conversation, focus on your listener. Ask questions and listen to the responses.

• Ask questions, lots of questions.

• Use open-ended questions.

• Rephrase questions or responses for the listener to ensure shared understanding.

• Offer alternatives/suggestions for the listener to evaluate.

• Define terminology so there is less chance of misunderstanding.

....

Andrew Bierce describes a bore as a person who talks when you want him to listen.

PART I–COMMUNICATION–TECHNIQUES

DEFINE ACRONYMS

Acronyms can have several meanings. Their meaning depends on the community in which they are used. Acronyms are used as words but are composed of the first letter or letters of a series of words. For example, the LOC (pronounced lock) at the Pentagon stands for Logistics Operations Center. People who work there or do business with the Center know this. But to the average person, "lock" has a different meaning.

- Use acronyms sparingly because they are not clearly understood by everyone. Acronyms are sometimes referred to as "alphabet soup."

- To ensure clear communication, say the acronym, then define it, as appropriate.

- Be sensitive to your listener's ability to understand your message.

EXAMPLE:
She is briefing the EUP in the LOC
for the DCSLOG at 0600.

TRANSLATION:
She is briefing the Equipment Usage
Profile in the Logistics Operations
Center for the Deputy Chief of Staff
for Logistics at 6:00 a.m.

PART I-COMMUNICATION-TECHNIQUES

REDUCE JARGON

Using jargon, much like acronyms, can seem exclusionary because it keeps some people out of the conversation. Thus, these terms should be used sparingly. If the listener has to think about your meaning, you run the risk of a misunderstanding.

• Use jargon, more popularly known as "shop talk," sparingly to ensure that your message is understood and that everyone involved is included rather than excluded.

• Slow down your rate of speech when using jargon and check the visual feedback for clues that others are understanding your meaning.

••

You can have brilliant ideas, but if you can't get them across, your ideas won't get you anywhere.

–Lee Iacocca

PART I–COMMUNICATION–TECHNIQUES

LEVEL OBJECTIONS

In conversations, there can be perception problems and hidden agendas. To become an effective communicator, we need to be aware of and avoid the potential barriers that may hamper our communications.

- Overcome communication barriers through active thinking and listening.

- Evaluate the other person's point of view. Avoid quick judgments.

- Handle controversy and challenges with fairness. Try to see the other point of view, even if you don't agree with it.

- Understand that objections are most often directed to a point made in the conversation and are not a personal attack.

- Control your emotions. When you lose emotional control, you've weakened your position.

- Make every encounter a win-win situation.

- In some cases preempt the anticipated objection by stating it. Then give reasons that support your points and overcome the objection.

PART I–COMMUNICATION–TECHNIQUES

USE HUMOR

Humor breaks down barriers. Humor relaxes. Humor makes us more receptive to others.

• Move on in your conversation if a bit of humor or a joke falls flat. Avoid lengthy explanations. Instead, focus on the point you want to make.

• Avoid giving the impression or stating that you expect laughter.

• Focus on the humorous aspects (or the lighter side) of your work.

• Use spontaneous humor by taking advantage of the situation at hand.

• Accumulate humorous material such as jokes, cartoons, and notes.

• Write down humorous things that happen to you and around you and record them in your humor journal for future retelling, including the point you want to make.

• Avoid using humor at another's expense.

• Use self-deprecating humor, and tell a joke on yourself occasionally.

• Use humor to make a point. Laughter is a plus.

• Laugh at your own jokes. It's okay.

PART I–COMMUNICATION–TECHNIQUES

USE ANECDOTES AND STORIES

Anecdotes are biographical incidents. Usually listeners will identify with the stories you tell and a common understanding results.

• Give an example by relating an incident which supports your point.

• Elaborate and add color by telling a short story.

• Use personal stories whenever possible rather than someone else's story.

• Avoid stories that degrade others.

• Use gender neutral language when possible.

• Use short, rather than longer, descriptive stories.

• Use anecdotes and stories that are generally understood by everyone.

••

Peter Drucker claims that 60 percent of all management problems result from faulty communications.

PART I–COMMUNICATION–TECHNIQUES

ASK FOR FEEDBACK

Our statements can be confusing. Feedback from our listener provides clarification.

• Ask the listener general questions, "Did I explain myself clearly?" or "Am I making this easy to follow?"

• Ask the listener specific questions to ensure the listener understands what you are saying. You might say, "What I hear you telling me is...Is that correct?"

• Offer further explanation to correct a misinterpretation.

PART I–COMMUNICATION–TECHNIQUES

INCREASE YOUR VOCABULARY

Using precise vocabulary words is like fine tuning a musical instrument. It is done in small increments. You won't learn many new words overnight, but with continued awareness and practice, you will expand your vocabulary over time.

• Listen to vocabulary tapes.

• Hear the correct pronunciation of words with which you are not familiar.

• Repeat the words aloud.

• Compare the way the words sound when you say them and the taped sounds.

• Continue to practice saying the words aloud, using them in a sentence.

• Carry vocabulary cards in your pocket or purse and practice while you are in transit, e.g., on the bus or an airplane.

• Read popular magazines and complete the word teasers.

• Do crossword puzzles.

• Circle words you don't understand when you are reading. Then look them up in the dictionary.

The difference between the right word and the almost right word is the difference between the lightening and the lightening bug.
–Mark Twain

PART I–COMMUNICATION–TECHNIQUES

ELIMINATE AUDIBLE PAUSES

Audible pauses, such as "ah," "er," "um," and other verbal fluff, obscure your message and reduce your credibility.

• Stop, think, then talk.

• Use shorter sentences.

• Substitute silence for audible pauses.

• Eliminate the reasons for audible pauses:

  -Lack of familiarity with the topic.

  -Discomfort with silence. (Pauses are very effective when used well and will help with discomfort by taking a moment to think about what you will say next.)

  -Nervousness.

  -Habit.

• Practice, practice, practice.

• Record yourself and listen for the audible pauses. Over a period of time, you should see improvement.

••

Audible pauses are like background music that is too loud.
–Kathi Bough

PART I–COMMUNICATION–TECHNIQUES

ENUNCIATE CLEARLY

When you enunciate your words clearly, no matter how softly or loudly you speak, the listener will be able to understand you. (For example, how many times have you listened to your voice mail and had to replay it to understand the message or get the phone number?)

• Record yourself and listen to the playback.

• Enunciate clearly:

  -You will clear up misunderstandings and misinterpretations.

  -Those who speak with an accent will be better understood.

• Breathe deeply and you are less likely to mumble.

• Note which words or sounds need to be clearer.

• Listen to radio and television announcers who usually have good diction.

• Put a cork between your teeth and repeat words which you do not articulate clearly.

....

Demosthenes, the great Greek orator, practiced speaking with pebbles in his mouth to improve his enunciation.

PART I-COMMUNICATION-TECHNIQUES

PRACTICE PRONOUNCING WORDS PROPERLY

Learning to pronounce words properly is the first step. The second important step is to put learning into action.

- Observe your facial movements by standing in front of a mirror as you pronounce difficult words.

- Listen to the sound of difficult words as you say them aloud to yourself.

- Listen to the words correctly pronounced by someone else. For example:

  -Play tapes.

  -Listen to television or radio programs where proper English is spoken.

- Pronounce words correctly for clarity and better understanding. (Avoid having to repeat.) Mispronunciation reduces credibility.

....

I'll pay more for a man's ability to express himself than for any other quality he might possess.
                                    –Charles Schwab

PART I–COMMUNICATION–TECHNIQUES

EXERCISE TONGUE, JAWS, LIPS

Exercise by exaggerating your words and sounds. This exercise releases tension, improves articulation, aids in developing natural facial expressions and strengthens the spoken word.

- Concentrate on the effect of your tongue, jaws, and lips when you articulate words.

- Exercise tongue, jaws, and lips in private.

- Exercise in front of a mirror so you can watch yourself improve.

- Exaggerate the articulation of your words and become comfortable with the changes you see and hear.

Your voice is the sound of your soul.

–Arthur Joseph

PART I–COMMUNICATION–TECHNIQUES

MAKE EYE CONTACT

When talking to someone, it is essential to have good eye contact to get accurate feedback on nonverbal cues. Confident eye contact generally indicates honesty and trustworthiness.

• Show interest by good eye contact.

• In formal speaking, focus eye-to-eye contact for three to five seconds then shift to another person.

• In informal situations, one-to-one and group situations, eye contact can be longer. The key is to avoid prolonged eye contact which can increase people's discomfort level.

• Adjust your conversation, as necessary, to meet the feedback you receive. For example, if you receive a quizzical look, clarify your points or ask questions to ensure that the person understands your message.

....

People from other cultures have varying beliefs about the use of eye contact. Be careful not to judge too quickly if someone from another country does not meet your eyes as you would expect an American to do.

PART I–COMMUNICATION–TECHNIQUES

GESTURE

Gestures include facial expressions, hand and body movements which accompany spoken and unspoken words. These gestures make conversations more lively and act as punctuation marks.

- Use deliberate facial, hand, or body movements to support or emphasize your oral message. This gives listeners additional clues to your meaning.

- Express your emotions with gestures.

Successful speaking lies in the eloquence and grace of physical movement.

–Larry Welch

PART I–COMMUNICATION–TECHNIQUES

PAUSE

Remember the advertisement, "the pause that refreshes?" This certainly applies to conversations. The pause allows the listener to relax, think and absorb your information. It also gives the listener the opportunity to participate in the conversation. Pauses are powerful. But exercise caution. Silence is not always golden. A prolonged pause can be unnerving.

- Create a pause:

  -Stop talking.

  -Think of what you will say next.

- Emphasize a point by pausing either before or after making the point.

- Pause to give your listener time to:

  -Participate in the conversation.

  -Think about what you are saying.

- Avoid rushing in to interrupt a pause created by someone else.

- Pause to give yourself time to collect your thoughts or emotions.

Silence is as full of potential wisdom and wit as the unhewn marble of great sculpture.

–Aldous Huxley

PART I–COMMUNICATION–TECHNIQUES

SPEAK MORE SLOWLY

By speaking too fast and tripping over words, you risk the possibility that your listeners will misunderstand what you have to say or get tired listening to you. But use caution. If you speak too slowly for any length of time, it could seem to indicate you lack energy or interest.

• Emphasize a point by slowing down.

• Vary your rate of speech. This demonstrates confidence and poise. It also increases the likelihood of clear communications.

• Slow down. This will give your listener an opportunity to think about and process what you are saying.

• React to verbal and nonverbal feedback from your listeners by speaking more slowly if it appears they are having difficulty understanding you.

PART I–COMMUNICATION–TECHNIQUES

SPEAK FASTER

The average listener processes information at a rate of 400-600 words per minute! By speaking faster, it indicates energy, enthusiasm and excitement.

• Hold your listener's attention by varying the pace of your speech. Speed up and slow down. The normal pace is about 125 to 150 words per minute.

• Increase your pace if your listener seems to be losing interest.

• Increase your pace to avoid droning. Besides putting people to sleep, droning makes you appear dull.

• Add variety to your communications by varying the pace of your talking from time to time.

• Continue to enunciate clearly.

PART I–COMMUNICATION–TECHNIQUES

VARY YOUR VOLUME

Lowering and raising your voice is like using punctuation marks. It holds the attention of your listener.

- Add spice and variety to the conversation.

- Take one word or phrase and explore the meaning by varying your vocal range.

- Use volume for emphasis.

- Practice modulating your voice from soft to loud to soft again.

- Project your voice by increasing your volume.

Soft words are hard arguments.
                                                                    –Thomas Fuller

PART I–COMMUNICATION–TECHNIQUES

WATCH YOUR TONE

The tone of voice you use gives evidence of your feelings.

- Be aware of the tone of voice that you use with your listener.

- Soften your tone to show respect or affection.

- Guard against unwittingly revealing negative emotions. (Your tone reveals feelings such as impatience, anger or rejection.)

- If you feel you have left a negative impression and want to change it, say you want to change it.

EXAMPLE:
I didn't mean to sound so gruff. I do understand the circumstances that caused you to be late.

PART I–COMMUNICATION–TECHNIQUES

RECORD YOUR VOICE

One of the most effective ways to improve your communication skills is to record your thoughts verbally. Listening helps you to discover the "real you."

• Learn how you sound to others.

• Discover your vocal quality.

• Practice for an important conversation, presentation or interview.

• Ask permission to tape when you are in conversation with a trusted friend.

• Play the tape in private as an aid to improve your communication skills.

PART I–COMMUNICATION–LISTENING

PREPARE TO LISTEN

Active listening means giving nonverbal and sometimes verbal feedback to the speaker. Listening requires us to concentrate and participate in the conversation. Hearing refers to awareness of the sound of the other person talking without really processing what they are saying.

• Allow time to listen.

• Create a receptive frame of mind.

• Listen with eyes and ears.

• Eliminate potential distractions.

• Focus on active listening.

....

The first step toward innovation is getting into the habit of listening.
–Tom Peters

PART I–COMMUNICATION–LISTENING

FOCUS ON THE SPEAKER

Effective communication begins with total concentration on the speaker's verbal and nonverbal communications.

• Look at the person who is speaking to you.

• Guard against unnecessary distractions.

• Review mentally what the speaker is saying to enhance listening.

• Ask yourself questions so you are ready to respond to the speaker.

• Maintain open body language to encourage communication.

• Consider the background and experience level.

PART I–COMMUNICATION–LISTENING

SCREEN OUT DISTRACTIONS

Nothing you can do will make others feel more important than giving them your full attention.

- Turn off all distractions such as television, radio, beepers, and ignore the telephone.

- Focus on the person with whom you are communicating.

- Tune out background noises.

- When unavoidable interruptions occur, excuse yourself and show interest when you return.

PART I–COMMUNICATION–LISTENING

CONCENTRATE ON THE MESSAGE

When your mind wanders, the flow of the conversation or message is lost. Your listeners feel complimented when they know you have heard their message.

• Focus on the other person's message. Note their point of view.

• Avoid:

  -Premature conclusions.

  -Letting your mind wander while the other person is talking.

  -Biding your time until it is your turn to speak. (Thinking of what you are going to say next.)

• Review the other person's point of view mentally so you can respond or rephrase the message.

....

If there is any one secret of success, it lies in the ability to get the other person's point of view and see things from his angle as well as your own.

–Henry Ford

PART I–COMMUNICATION–LISTENING

LISTEN TO TAPES WHILE YOU COMMUTE

Learning organizations begin with people who are interested in a lifetime of learning. Time is precious. Commuting time can be made more productive by listening to tapes.

• Be open to learning.

• Select tapes that can help expand (improve) your mind.

• Broaden your intellect by:

  -Listening to books on tape.

  -Learning a different language.

  -Improving memory.

• Improve your mental attitude.

• Keep abreast of latest information.

• Increase knowledge in your field of expertise.

EXAMPLES:
Accelerated Learning
   by Brian Tracy
Mega Memory
   by Kevin Trudeau
Wordmaster
   by Denis Waitley &
   Achievement
   Technologies Corp.

PART I–COMMUNICATION–SPEAKING AND LISTENING

ASK QUESTIONS

Whether you are the speaker or a listener, asking questions facilitates an exchange of information.

- Ask questions of your listeners to:
  -Clarify your message.

  -Improve understanding.

  -Get deeper into the issues.

  -Discover motives.

- Show interest by asking questions of the speaker's ideas and experiences.

- Avoid questions that pry into personal matters. Be sensitive.

- When asking questions, frame them tactfully.

- Avoid challenging the listener's questions and recognize the consequences if you do. You may

  -Stop flow of information.

  -Offend or hurt feelings.

He who is afraid to ask is ashamed of learning.
–Ancient Proverb

PART I-COMMUNICATION-SPEAKING AND LISTENING

AVOID DAYDREAMING

Daydreaming is normal because of listener's spare time. We process information at about 400-600 words per minute while the average speaking range is from 125-150 words per minute. The difference is listener's spare time. To avoid daydreaming:

• Focus on your speaker.

• Listen to your speaker and interact by actively giving the speaker verbal and nonverbal feedback. Use such nonverbal cues as nodding or smiling.

• Concentrate on the speaker's point of view; review or mentally check to see if you are in agreement.

• As a speaker, reduce listener's spare time by use of vocal and visual cues as well as use of stories, anecdotes, humor, and metaphors.

....

There is a time and place for daydreaming such as a lead into visualization, creative imagination or just plain relaxation.

PART I–COMMUNICATION–SPEAKING AND LISTENING

ACCEPT ACCENTS

• Accents are regarded by some as charming. They're okay.

• Recognize the value of accents (individuality).

• Accept individual differences.

• Listen attentively.

• Concentrate to understand.

• If you have an accent and it is a natural part of your personality:

  -Avoid being overly concerned about eliminating the accent.

  -Concentrate on communication techniques such as slowing down, enunciating, and pronouncing words.

A Gallop Poll communication survey related that among the things Americans found annoying only 24% found regional or foreign accents annoying. Compare that to 61% who found a high-pitched voice annoying, and 88% who found interrupting while others talked annoying.

PART I–COMMUNICATION–SPEAKING AND LISTENING

USE MIND MAPPING

Mind Mapping is a system of recording our thoughts so that we employ both left brain and right brain thinking, i.e., whole brain thinking. In order to do this, we use key words, symbols and color. Mind Mapping allows us to generate and organize thoughts at the same time.

• Write down a main point, central thought or idea.

• Circle the main thought, then use interconnecting branches to show associated ideas.

• In note taking, mind map things you are thinking about. You will generate more ideas, see relationships among key words, write less than in conventional note taking; and have more fun!

• In making telephone calls, mind map who you are going to call, your purpose for calling, when you intend to call, what questions you want answered or what comments you want to make, and what information you want to share.

Dilip Abayasekara, Ph.D.

PART I–COMMUNICATION–SPEAKING AND LISTENING

INTERVIEW

Whether you are the interviewer or the interviewee, you will have a stake in the successful outcome of the encounter.

• Think ahead.

• Prepare for the interview by gathering information about the topic and the other person(s) who will be participating in, or affected by, the interview.

• Make a list of questions you want to ask and information you need to acquire during the interview.

• Listen carefully for points you didn't think of before.

• Look pleasant; smile when appropriate.

• Stay actively engaged in the interview; guard against distractions.

• Take notes; use mind-mapping techniques.

....

Enthusiasm is the key to enjoying interviewing and conducting effective interviews, at any level.

–Richard Nelson Bolles

PART I–COMMUNICATION–SPEAKING AND LISTENING

COMPLAINTS

When we're not satisfied with products or services, we can improve our chances for satisfactory results by using effective communication techniques.

• State the problem.

• Supply supporting evidence.

• State the remedy you seek. What do you want done about it?

• Hold your temper.

• Avoid attacking the person listening to your complaint.

• Let them know when you want corrective action completed.

• Ask to see the supervisor or the manager when the person you are speaking with is unable to help you.

• As a last resort, tell them other approaches you plan to take to get resolution of the problem, such as taking your complaint to the manufacturer or getting media attention.

PART I–COMMUNICATION–SPEAKING AND LISTENING

TELEPHONE

The telephone is the most common way of communicating with people on a daily basis. The results depend on your use of communication techniques specifically for the telephone whether you are placing or receiving a call.

• Organize your thoughts before you place the call.

• Put a smile in your voice by putting a smile on your face.

• Avoid lengthy, preachy announcements to callers when they reach your voice mail.

• Be prepared to leave a message if you receive voice mail.

• Time your business calls to avoid rambling.

• Leave messages that facilitate action. Before you call:

  -Know what outcome you want.
  -Mind-map or outline your message with bullet points.

• Record on voice mail the following:

  -Date and time of your call.
  -Name and phone number (enunciate clearly!).
  -Your message.

PART I–COMMUNICATION–SPEAKING AND LISTENING

ATTEND A TOASTMASTERS MEETING

Toastmasters International is a non-profit educational organization dedicated to improving communication and leadership skills. A Toastmaster meeting serves as a laboratory for improving communication skills. At each meeting, members present prepared speeches and receive feedback with recommendations for improvements. In this environment, members improve their speaking, thinking and listening skills.

• Learn by observing other people practicing their communication skills.

• Listen for tips for improvement given as feedback to speakers that might apply to you as well.

• Receive constructive feedback on your speeches.

• Talk with a Toastmaster or a former Toastmaster about the value of becoming a member of a Toastmasters club.

To continue to improve your speaking, thinking, and listening skills, join a Toastmasters club.
For a small fee you can become a member and begin practicing in a supportive, compassionate environment immediately.

PART II–SPEAKING AND WRITING–KEY POINTS

WRITE A PURPOSE STATEMENT

A purpose statement helps you to think through what you are going to say and stay focused on the essential message. It sets your parameters.

- Write a one-sentence purpose statement before you begin to write, whether it is a letter, thesis or speech.

- Use the who, what, where, when and how format to keep your message focused and brief.

- Write and rewrite until you are able to capture the idea in one sentence.

....

The secret of success is constancy to purpose.
                                        –Benjamin Disraeli

PART II–SPEAKING AND WRITING–KEY POINTS

USE AN OUTLINE

An outline helps you to organize your thoughts before speaking or writing. As the creative juices flow, jot down ideas, then go back and sort them.

• Make notes of what you want to say in outline form.

   1. List all major points or topics you want to address or cover.

   2. List supporting points.

      a. Give necessary details.

      b. Provide examples or anccdotes.

• Repeat this process until your entire message is covered.

• Arrange in a logical sequence, such as order of importance.

• Review and reshuffle points until they make the best impact.

PART II–SPEAKING AND WRITING–KEY POINTS

TRANSFER NEGATIVE EMOTIONS TO PAPER

Writing out your negative emotions on paper releases some emotional stress. Write out what you want to say especially when strong emotions are involved, or when there is the potential for a lasting negative impact.

• Sort out your issues and emotions.

• Keep your emotions under control.

• Put your anger on paper or into the computer but **do not send the document.** This gives you an opportunity to vent your hostility without doing permanent damage.

• Ask yourself, "If the intended recipient had this information, would it be to my advantage?"

• Set aside your writing and return to it after a "cooling off" period.

• Consider asking someone else who is not involved in the issue to listen to you, read what you wrote and provide objective feedback before a confrontation.

• Destroy anything you have written in anger. Let some time pass and begin again.

···

When angry, count to ten before you speak (or write), if very angry, one hundred.

–Thomas Jefferson

PART II–SPEAKING AND WRITING–KEY POINTS

GET TO THE POINT QUICKLY

Know what you want to say, say it quickly and get to the point. Rambling is a barrier to effective listening. People will not listen to you unless you get to the point quickly.

• Answer the question, "What is my point?"

• Put your major point or request, your "bottom line," first.

• Avoid the risk that your listener or reader will be interrupted or simply tune you out before you get to your major point or request.

• In closing, reiterate your point(s).

PART II–SPEAKING AND WRITING–KEY POINTS

EXPLAIN ABSTRACT WORDS

When using abstract words make the idea more tangible. For example, "strong as an ox."

- Use a metaphor, e.g., "he plows through his work."

- Restate the idea using different words.

- Paint a picture to clarify the abstract term such as the word "conversation," e.g., "A conversation is like a tennis match where the listener and speaker are the players."

- Use a simile, e.g., "Her teeth are like pearls."

Metaphor implies one thing is like another. "But meaning is an arrow that reaches its mark when least encumbered with feathers." Herbert Read, English Prose Style.

Simile says one thing is like another using the words "like" or "as": She was as graceful as a willow tree.

PART II–SPEAKING AND WRITING–KEY POINTS

USE ABSOLUTES AND GENERALITIES SPARINGLY

Absolutes and generalities are difficult to explain or defend. Generalities weaken our statements; absolutes are dogmatic statements which often cannot be proven. These terms have exclusive properties which are barriers to effective communications, e.g., "I never...We always...." The use of these terms may indicate a lack of understanding or may show poor preparation for discussing a particular topic.

• Avoid using absolutes and generalities.

• Explain why you are using absolutes or generalities. It shows you are aware of the word's properties and are using them for a specific purpose.

• When using absolutes or generalities, avoid assuming that your listener agrees with your statement.

EXAMPLES:
    Absolute: Texans are always
                friendly.
    Generality: Everybody believes that
                Texans think they have
                the biggest of
                everything.

PART II–SPEAKING AND WRITING–KEY POINTS

ASK FOR WHAT YOU WANT

Ask for what you want, thoughtfully and tactfully. Begin by making small requests. Success builds on success. Every success reduces the fear of rejection when you next ask for what you want.

• Make your requests as specific as possible.

• Ask for information.

• Ask for help first from those closest to you. They are more likely to give a positive response.

• Guard against feeling rejected when the request you make is not granted.

• Expect a favorable reply.

• Visualize yourself receiving what you ask for.

• Formulate positive affirmations and repeat them aloud to yourself to develop a belief that you shall have what you ask for.

• Remember to say "Thank you."

RESOURCE:
The Aladdin Factor
by Jack Canfield &
Mark Victor Hansen

Ask and you shall receive, seek and you will find, and knock and it shall be opened to you..

–Holy Bible, Matt 7:7

PART II–SPEAKING AND WRITING–KEY POINTS

USE ACTIVE VERBS

Active verbs add more power and energy to your communication.

• State the doer of the action before the action is done.

• Add clarity to your sentence.

• Use passive voice only occasionally, for variety.

• Assign responsibility for action.

EXAMPLES:
Active: Jane prepared the sales
         presentation.
Passive: The sales presentation
         was prepared by Jane.

PART II–SPEAKING AND WRITING–KEY POINTS

USE GENDER NEUTRAL LANGUAGE

Sexist language immediately raises resentment in many people. To hold the attention of all your listeners, include everyone in your comments. Although "he" is still universal, overuse sounds exclusive.

- Use the plural instead of singular pronouns, "their" instead of "his or hers."

- Formulate sentences without pronouns, "Everyone is expected to do the job well," instead of "his or her job."

- Be consistent in addressing women and men of the same rank or status. Frequently, women are addressed by their first names while men are called "Mr. Surname".

- Use gender neutral terminology. For instance, use "work force" instead of "manpower."

- Provide guidance for both sexes on invitations; e.g., "business attire" instead of "coat and tie."

....

Prejudices...are most difficult to eradicate
from the heart whose soil has never been
loosened or fertilized by education;
they grow there, firm as weeds among stones.

–Charlotte Bronte

PART II–SPEAKING AND WRITING–KEY POINTS.

CITE THE SOURCE OF STATISTICAL DATA

Citing the source indicates you are prepared, that you know your subject well and are willing to give credit. By stating your source, you will reduce the likelihood of a challenge.

• Check to be sure you are correct.

• Be precise in your statement.

• When providing statistical data in written form, indicate the date as well as the source of the material.

• Refer to your source.

EXAMPLE:
According to the Gallop Poll
communication study...

PART II–SPEAKING AND WRITING–KEY POINTS

ILLUSTRATE WITH PERSONAL EXAMPLES

People think in pictures, not words. Using personal examples helps people to relate quickly to your message without spending too much time mentally translating your message into a picture.

- Help people to relate to you by sharing personal experiences.

- Build a source of personal examples by keeping a journal.

- Use stories from your past to illustrate the point or the message you want to leave with your listeners.

PART II–SPEAKING AND WRITING–KEY POINTS

EXPRESS EMOTION

Emotion should be an aid to understanding. It allows others to empathize with us.

- Describe feelings as well as facts.

- Set limits. Extreme emotion becomes a barrier.

- Indicate that you are approachable.

- Use body language as a part of your emotional expression.

....

...with sound, the emotion communicates the idea, which is more direct and therefore more powerful.

–Alfred North Whitehead

See also "suppress emotions, p59."

PART II–SPEAKING AND WRITING–KEY POINTS

KEEP IT SIMPLE

Short and simple sentences aid the listener's understanding.

• If you use abstract reasoning, be sure your listeners understand. Ask for feedback.

• Rephrase the same idea in a different way.

• Match your vocabulary with the comprehension level of your listener.

• Avoid trying to impress others by using big words.

....

Short words are best and the old words when short are best of all.

–Winston Churchill

PART II–SPEAKING AND WRITING–KEY POINTS

PAINT VERBAL PICTURES

People think in pictures, not words. Help your listeners see what you mean. Everyone processes information primarily through one preferred sensory channel. By referring to different channels, everyone's preferred mode is included.

• Use descriptions with colors, smells, and feelings.

• Use metaphors and similes.

• Use stories and anecdotes to enrich your message.

• Employ as many sensory channels (sight, touch, smell, sound, taste) as possible.

Your words are the clothes that thoughts wear, so dress them well.

–Anonymous

PART II–SPEAKING AND WRITING–KEY POINTS

BE CONCISE

Being concise adds clarity, crispness, and power to your message. You will catch the listener's attention more quickly. Concise sentences are easier to read.

- Choose words carefully. Sometimes one word can replace several providing greater impact.

- Keep your message focused.

One way to cut down on paperwork is to learn to say things in fewer words.

–Joe Griffith

PART II–SPEAKING AND WRITING–KEY POINTS

SUPPORT STATEMENTS WITH DETAILS

In talking with others be prepared to give more details, or cut back on details, depending on the listener's nonverbal cues.

• Put your most important statement first and follow it with supporting material.

• Give additional facts and figures for greater credibility.

• Watch the listener for nonverbal cues on how much detail is needed to support your message.

• Anticipate questions from the listener's nonverbal cues and be prepared to provide additional information.

EXAMPLE:
I had a great day today!
The boss gave me a raise and
my associate sent me flowers!

PART II–SPEAKING AND WRITING–KEY POINTS

WATCH SEMANTICS

The meaning of a word may vary according to the way it is used in a given situation. The speaker or writer could use a word intending a specific meaning, but the listener or reader may give the word a different interpretation. It is important to have a common understanding of the word.

• Know when your words might have double meanings. Clarify as needed.

• Ask for feedback to ensure the message is received as you intended.

Nothing gives us away more to others than the way we speak.

–Earl Nightingale.

PART II–SPEAKING AND WRITING–KEY POINTS

QUOTE AUTHORITIES

Quoting authorities gives evidence that you are abreast of current thinking on a subject. Giving the source of a quote demonstrates personal credibility.

• Add additional strength to your point.

• Do your homework. Read and listen to recognized experts and others in your field.

• State your own opinions and conclusions along with the quote.

• Use quotations to support the point as needed. Overuse of quotations may give the impression that you have few ideas of your own.

....

If I have seen further, it is because I have stood on the shoulders of giants.

–Sir Isaac Newton

PART II–SPEAKING AND WRITING–KEY POINTS

CONSULT EXPERTS

Consult experts on your topic. This adds credibility and depth to your message.

• Find opportunities to meet leaders in your field.

• Be prepared to gain knowledge from chance encounters with the experts.

• Soon after your encounter make note of the speaker, date and occasion as well as pertinent information you wish to quote.

• Support your statements with specific facts you can attribute to an expert.

• Get permission from the expert if you want to quote in print, "I am doing research on this topic. May I quote you?"

....

In the first five seconds, your audience judges you on your appearance, your body language, your voice, your message, and how you handle the media.
–Lillian Brown
Author, *YOUR PUBLIC BEST: The Complete Guide to Making Successful Public Appearances*

PART II–SPEAKING AND WRITING–KEY POINTS

SUPPRESS EMOTION

There are appropriate times to express your emotions and times to suppress your emotions. It is important to remain in control of your emotions to maintain objectivity.

• Know when to express and when to suppress emotion.

• To regain control of your own emotions, take deep breaths, exhaling slowly.

• Express strong emotions such as anger with discretion.

• Avoid expressing intense emotions which tend to cloud reasoning and decrease credibility.

• •

[Beware of emotionally charged words.]
...those whose sense may be distorted by preconceived adverse reactions. Words such as agitator, demagogue, and politician have feelings associated with their meanings and express or appeal to emotion.

–Thomas Montalbo

PART II–SPEAKING AND WRITING–WRITING

KEEP A JOURNAL

Journaling is recording thoughts, ideas, and feelings, in writing, on a daily basis. Over time it comprises our personal history and a reference point for reviewing our progress toward a goal. It helps us sort out and draw conclusions from things that occur to us.

- Use a bound book with lined paper to get started.

- Relax in a peaceful place and let your thoughts flow in quiet reflection.

- Write whatever comes to mind for a specific time. This is called "free writing."

- Slow down and organize your thoughts.

- Think about what you are writing. Look for connections.

- Reexamine the things you were taught as a child. Then analyze how your values and convictions have changed—-or not.

....

Writing down your thoughts enables you not only to chart where you are going, it helps you to clearly remember where you've been and credit yourself for how far you've come.

–Randyl "Blake" Mitchell

PART II–SPEAKING AND WRITING–WRITING

TAKE NOTES

During business meetings and at other times when you need to remember something, note taking is invaluable.

- Know what is important and what is not.

- Ask questions when you are in doubt.

- Record new ideas and those items on which you must take action.

- After you first meet someone, take a moment and jot down key information about the person and the conversation.

- Spell the person's name phonetically so that you remember how to pronounce it. If you know how, also spell it correctly.

He listens well who takes notes.

–Dante

PART II–SPEAKING AND WRITING–WRITING

WRITE PERSONAL NOTES

Unexpected notes to friends, acquaintances, and family members uplift your spirits and those of the recipient.

- Keep in touch. Periodically say "hello" with a quick note.

- Set aside time to write. Early morning works well for many. Usually there is no interference and thoughts flow freely.

- Find a good place to write and use it consistently.

- Keep a supply of stationery and note cards at hand.

- Plan to write three to five notes daily.

- Tell how you feel about situations and events.

- Acknowledge gifts and favors with a thank you note sent within a week of the occasion.

- Use postcards occasionally except for information which should be kept private.

PART II–SPEAKING AND WRITING–WRITING

WRITE MORE EFFECTIVE BUSINESS LETTERS

A business letter is a reflection on the professionalism of a person or organization. It enhances or diminishes the possibility of achieving the desired results.

• Think before you write.

• Put your major point in the first paragraph.

• Use active verbs. The subject of the sentence is the actor, e.g., "The director chaired the meeting," instead of "The meeting was chaired by the director."

• Avoid stilted and formal writing.

• Address the person by name in the body of the letter as well as at the beginning.

• Use personal pronouns.

• In writing about situations or events, use words that describe what you see, hear, touch, smell, and taste.

• Revise.

....

Thinking is the activity I love best, and writing is simply thinking through my fingers.

–Issac Asimov

PART II–SPEAKING AND WRITING–WRITING

USE SHORT SENTENCES

Shorter sentences pack more power. They are also easier to read and understand.

• Avoid run-on, rambling sentences.

• Review your written work and see if conjunctions can be deleted to form two sentences. (Example: Review your written work. See if conjunctions can be deleted to form two sentences.)

The ability to simplify means to eliminate the unnecessary so that the necessary may speak.

–Hans Hoffman

PART II–SPEAKING AND WRITING–WRITING

COMMUNICATE ONLINE

Electronic mail (e-mail) is a quick way to send a message to one or more people if you have a computer. The receiver, however, may not open the e-mail for several hours or days. Anything you send in e-mail or on the internet should be considered public information.

• Subscribe to an online service such as America Online, Juno, or CompuServe.

• Learn to use e-mail. You can also communicate through newsgroups, chat rooms, and bulletin boards.

• Compose letters for e-mail with salutation and complimentary close.

• Compose and edit off line.

• Be concise; get to the point quickly.

• Learn about "netiquette," the customs and manners involved in using on line services. For example, the use of all capital letters indicates that you are shouting.

....

Among many sources,
The Official America Online for Windows Tour Guide and
Fabrik's e-mail Netiquette Guide
at www.fabrik.com

PART III–GENERAL TIPS–READING

READ

Many of us do not read because it is time consuming, quiet work. Others have discovered the joy of sharing in solitude someone else's ideas and adventures. Reading helps us become better educated and better conversationalists.

• Make reading a habit. Set aside time every day to read.

• Scan the material or the table of contents.

• Skim to pick up major points.

• Focus on the main theme.

• Read to learn; read to enjoy.

If someone you know wants improved reading skills, recommend:
-Adult education courses in reading.
-The Literacy Council
-The local library

PART III–GENERAL TIPS–READING

KEEP UP TO DATE WITH CURRENT EVENTS

There are many sources to keep you informed: newspapers, magazines, television, radio, the internet, as well as the people and events around us.

- Question the intent of the reporter. Over time you may learn of a reporter's bias toward various topics.

- Think as you read or listen. You are not required to accept everything as factual.

- Find another article or program about the same event and see it from another reporter's point of view.

- Discuss current events with your acquaintances.

- Do not expect everyone to interpret events in the same way.

- Scan even the sections of newspapers and magazines that you are not particularly interested in, e.g., sports, finance, arts.

....

Let us dare to read, think, speak, and write...Let every sluice of knowledge be opened and set a-flowing.

–John Adams

PART III-GENERAL TIPS-READING

READ SOMETHING INSPIRATIONAL

Books like the Bible and the Koran not only give us guidelines for living; they also soothe the soul. They provide resources to draw upon for information or consolation.

• Read inspirational books.

• Subscribe to newsletters or pamphlets which provide regular readings to lift the spirit.

• Begin to form a habit of regularly reading inspirational thoughts and verses.

• Carry an inspirational verse with you to reflect upon during spare moments when you are caught in traffic or are standing in line.

• Check internet sources for inspirational messages.

• Read or write poetry that inspires you.

....

One ought every day at least, to hear a little song, read a good poem, see a fine picture, and, if it were possible, to speak a few reasonable words.

–Johann von Goethe

PART III–GENERAL TIPS–READING

USE THE INTERNET

Too much information can be as bad as not enough. Distilling it to make it useful is the key.

• Learn about resources such as America Online's Gopher and WAIS (Wide Area Information Server), and Netscape's Yahoo, for starters.

   -Gopher finds things on the internet and
    displays nested menus. Good for browsing.

   -WAIS uses query forms and is better suited for
    searching when you know what you want and where
    it may be.

   -ALEX is a catalog of electronic texts. Access
    is through Gopher's main category "Literature
    and Publications."

   -Yahoo is an internet directory on Netscape.

Reference:
The Internet for Busy People,
by Christian Crumlish

PART III–GENERAL TIPS–NONVERBAL

PRESENCE

Presence signals an individual's personal power. It exudes strength, awareness and confidence.

- Be aware of who you are, the role you play, and who your audience is.

- Be "in the moment" and in tune with your inner self.

- Exude strength and awareness through confidence and poise.

- Sit and stand erect.

- Let your nonverbal cues reflect the message you want to convey.

- Signal your self-esteem and power.

- Draw attention to yourself in a positive way.

- Let your body language agree with your spoken words.

- Realize that others are getting an impression of you during the first visual or verbal contact.

PART III–GENERAL TIPS–NONVERBAL

GIVE NONVERBAL CUES

Nonverbal cues enhance communications. Our body language says many things to other people.

- Use nonverbal communications intentionally to signal active listening.

  -Lean toward the speaker to show interest.

  -Smile to indicate you are receptive to their ideas.

  -Nod your head to indicate agreement.

  -Be subtle. Overdoing it will detract.

- If you are puzzled by nonverbal clues, keep looking or ask tactfully for an explanation.

- Notice your place at a conference table. It may indicate your rank in the organization or meeting.

  -The more powerful person takes up more space.

  -The head or the center of the table is usually reserved for the one in charge or the Chair of the meeting.

  -A round table signifies that attendees are of equal importance.

PART III–GENERAL TIPS–NONVERBAL

CHECK YOUR POSTURE

Posture is a nonverbal cue. Erect posture projects confidence, leadership, and authority.

- Sit and stand erect. This projects confidence and authority.

- Realize that first impressions are affected by your posture.

- Practice good posture when you are alone so it becomes natural.

- Do deep breathing exercises. You will be less likely to slump.

If you are physically unable to sit or stand erect, other clues, such as the tone of your voice, can also indicate your confidence and authority.

PART III–GENERAL TIPS–NONVERBAL

DRESS APPROPRIATELY

When you know you look good, you feel good about your-self. When you dress appropriate to the occasion, you are not drawing attention to yourself. Your listener will think, consciously or subconsciously, that you are "one of us." This aids communication.

- Find out what dress is considered appropriate. For example, attire that is acceptable in the Midwest may not be appropriate in the same situation in New York.

- Be sure your clothing sends the message you intend. Before you say a word, what you wear affects first impressions.

- Wear clothing that is congruent with your verbal message. If, for example, you are a business woman in a business situation, sheer, lacy blouses will not advance a serious message. Similarly, when everyone in the office is dressed in business attire and you show up in jeans and a tee-shirt, you are not in appropriate attire unless it's a day designated as "casual."

- Read a book on how to dress for various situations such as public appearances or business meetings.

PART III–GENERAL TIPS–NONVERBAL

SMILE

A smile is the most effective means to establish effective communications. It is a facial expression that signals you are pleased or happy. The corners of the mouth turn upward, the teeth are often seen as the lips are parted, and the eyes sparkle.

• Use a smile to signal that you are in a pleasant mood, positive, and approachable.

• Practice smiling in front of a mirror to gain confidence. See how you look with a broad smile showing your teeth, a smile with lips together, and a smile with teeth parted, possibly leading to a soft laugh.

• Smile to indicate a positive attitude:

 -Respect for the other person.

 -Friendliness.

 -Openness.

The smile must be of the right kind; and the right kind must have understanding in it, and friendliness, and a good deal of patience.
                                    –Roderic Owen

PART III–GENERAL TIPS–NONVERBAL

TOUCH

Touch is another sensory input which can aid communication. However, it must be done respectfully and with the other person's permission.

• Be sensitive to the fact that when you touch someone, you are invading their space.

• Use to indicate warmth, caring and understanding.

• Develop the techniques of proper touching:

  -Gently place your hand on the other person's arm between the elbow and the wrist in a friendly conversation.

  -Break contact immediately if there is any resistance.

  -Never use touch to enforce your will upon another person. That's against the law.

PART III–GENERAL TIPS–NONVERBAL

SHAKE HANDS PROPERLY

Important judgments are sometimes made based on a person's handshake.

• Grasp the other person's hand so that the skin at the base of your thumb touches that of the other person.

• Provide a firm and intentional shake and then release.

• Do not "strong arm" the other person. A handshake is not a test of strength and may create resentment if excessive force or squeezing is used.

• Practice with someone you know well if you are in doubt about the quality of your handshake.

PART III–GENERAL TIPS–ATTITUDE

INTEND TO IMPROVE

Set a goal to show improvement in a specific area of communication by a certain date. Expect to get results.

- Accept the fact that you can improve your communication skills.

- Get the thought of accomplishment into your subconscious mind.

- Change negative self-talk through awareness and positive affirmations.

- Add a statement to your affirmations with positive self-talk. The statement should indicate your expected outcome. It should be expressed as though it has been accomplished, e.g. "I have significantly improved my communication skills."

- Demonstrate an expected positive outcome.

- Learn and practice new techniques you find in this book to improve your ability to communicate.

....

What you can do or dream you can, begin it...Boldness has genius, power and magic in it.

–Johann von Goethe

PART III–GENERAL TIPS–ATTITUDE

VISUALIZE

Visualization is a technique of using your imagination to create what you want in your life.

• Find a restful place and become comfortable.

• Free your mind from worry and extraneous thoughts.

• Think about the outcome you want from reading this book. Create a clear picture in your mind. For example, see yourself as an effective, interesting communicator.

• Think positive thoughts about your communication skills.

• See yourself having already accomplished what you are starting out to do. Focus frequently on that idea or picture. Your subconscious mind cannot distinguish between what is real and what is vividly imagined.

• Embellish your thoughts with sounds, colors, smells, and textures.

• Develop positive statements or affirmations indicating that what you want already exists. This is similar to virtual reality in the business and military environments.

• Let yourself feel the exhilaration of success.

PART III–GENERAL TIPS–ATTITUDE

BE FLEXIBLE

Being flexible is part of the give and take of everyday living. It means bouncing back after being disappointed; being able to "get over it!" and move on.

• Be willing to relinquish control of the conversation.

• Listen to the other person's point of view.

• Be willing to change your mind.

• Be willing to compromise (if it's not a matter of principle).

• Be ready to state your point in a different, perhaps simpler, way to help the other person understand.

....

The weather-cock on the church spire, though made of iron, would soon be broken by the storm-wind if it...did not understand the noble art of turning to every wind.

–Heinrich Heine

PART III–GENERAL TIPS–ATTITUDE

BE LIKABLE

On first contact, the listeners will instantaneously make a judgment as to whether they like, trust, and believe the speaker. If listeners like the speaker, effective communication begins. The speaker's ideas immediately become more acceptable.

• Smile.

• Be friendly.

• Lower your defenses.

• Be aware of the other person's perception of you. How do you "come across?"

• To get what you want, look for points of agreement upon which you may build.

• Do not argue.

• Check your disposition. Are you predisposed to agree with the person with whom you are conversing? Or are you someone who instinctively tends to play Devil's Advocate?

....

I have learned from experience that the greater part of our happiness or misery depends on our dispositions and not on our circumstances.

–Martha Washington

PART III–GENERAL TIPS–ATTITUDE

COMMIT TO BEING TRUTHFUL

Credibility, once lost, is hard to regain. Your reputation may be at stake.

- Cultivate your image as morally trustworthy.

- Beware of half-truths, hidden agendas and ulterior motives

- Demonstrate respect for the other person.

- Be sensitive.

- Use tact. Do not abandon consideration of another's feelings. Truth has nothing to do with telling some one his tie is ugly.

- In social situations, silence may be the better choice in many cases.

....
*Time is precious, but truth
is more precious than time.*
—Benjamin Disraeli

PART III–GENERAL TIPS–ATTITUDE

EMPATHIZE

Mentally switch places with your listener. Listen to yourself as if you were in their place. Understanding the other person's viewpoint enables you to make your message easier to comprehend and accept.

• Be sensitive to the other person's situation.

• Speak in a language that is helpful and acceptable to the listener.

• Try to understand the other person's viewpoint.

THE PLATINUM RULE:
Do unto others as they'd like done unto them.
–Tony Alessandra, Ph.D.,
and Michael J. O'Connor, Ph.D.

PART III–GENERAL TIPS–ATTITUDE

DON'T TAKE YOURSELF TOO SERIOUSLY

When you can laugh at yourself, you become more human. Effective communication becomes easier. Humor can make a powerful point.

• Lighten up!

• Be willing to laugh. See the humor in situations.

• Be willing to concede a point.

• Do not take offense too quickly. Be sure you understand the message and the intent.

• Use self-deprecating humor. Occasionally "poke fun" at yourself.

• Look for humor in things that happen to you every day. Write them in your journal. Turn these happenings into stories to make your conversations more interesting.

. . . .

If you could choose one characteristic that would get you through life, choose a sense of humor.

–Jennifer Jones

PART III–GENERAL TIPS–ATTITUDE

ELIMINATE NEGATIVE FEELINGS

Negative feelings drain our energy. While they may be unavoidable at times to face injustice or for self-preservation, you should decide when such negative emotion is necessary. Generally, people tend to avoid those who habitually have negative attitudes.

• Gain control of your feelings.

• Be aware of your "self-talk." What are you silently saying to yourself?

• Negative feelings often carry over into conversations. Nonverbal signals may be incongruent with what you are trying to express.

• When negative feelings affect your self-confidence, practice positive self-talk. Develop a list of positive affirmations, with statements like

    I will . . .

    I can . . .

    I am . . .

....

Remember no one can make you feel inferior without your consent.

—Eleanor Roosevelt

PART III–GENERAL TIPS–ATTITUDE

BE RECEPTIVE TO NEW IDEAS

Often we concentrate so hard on getting our message across that we miss vital signals provided by the person with whom we are speaking.

• Relax and allow time for input.

• Listen attentively.

• Mentally examine what the other person is saying.

• Consider how the new ideas might apply to things you already know. They may add to your knowledge, encourage you to study further, or change your mind.

• Process information with an intent to find agreement.

• Yield control.

• Think before you speak.

....

A closed mind is a dying mind.
–Edna Ferber

PART III–GENERAL TIPS–ATTITUDE

TAKE RESPONSIBILITY

Take personal responsibility for effective communication.

- Take responsibility for what you say. If you're not sure of its accuracy, say so.

- If your listener is puzzled, ask "Am I not stating this clearly?" instead of "Why don't you understand what I said?"

- Acknowledge mistakes in communication, such as mispronunciation, and correct them as soon as possible.

- If you unintentionally offend someone, correct it and apologize on the spot.

PART III–GENERAL TIPS–ATTITUDE

RESPECT THE OTHER PERSON'S POINT OF VIEW

No two people are exactly alike. Building relationships requires us to exchange ideas, learn what we agree upon, and accept the fact that there will be differences of opinion.

• Try to understand why people think the way they do. What experience or learning has taken place that influences their thinking? Remember, you can understand another point of view without necessarily agreeing.

• When others are talking, dismiss minor deviations from your "truth" when they do not affect the outcome.

PART III–GENERAL TIPS–ATTITUDE

RECOGNIZE THE IMPACT OF STRESS ON COMMUNICATION

If you live or work in a high-stress environment, personal frustrations may block effective communication.

• Recognize the impact of frustration or stress on effective communication.

• Control your frustration level when surrounded by shouting, yelling, and screaming (for example, in a restaurant where several employees who are trying to be responsive to each other, and to the customers, get into a shouting match)

• Guard against being curt, impatient, or defensive.

• When people around you seem to lose control, be the "eye of the storm," and attempt to remain calm.

....

Nothing gives one person so much advantage over another as to remain always cool and unruffled under all circumstances.

–Thomas Jefferson

PART III–GENERAL TIPS–ATTITUDE

BE REAL

In an effort to have others accept us or our ideas, we often try to impress them by exaggerating our personality traits. In doing so, we overstate our positive points and leave a false impression of ourselves. Instead, build your confidence level. Let the "real you" come through to others.

• Allow people to get to know your likes, dislikes and beliefs.

• Determine the appropriate level of self-disclosure. What you might tell a person you know and like well, you probably would not tell to an acquaintance.

• Don't pretend to be something you are not. Dogs, babies, and adults can almost always sense a false front.

....

To thine own self be true.
And it must follow, as the
night the day, Thou canst
not then be false to any man.
–Shakespeare

PART III–GENERAL TIPS–ATTITUDE

CHECK YOUR ATTITUDE

Do people put up barriers when they see you coming? It could be that how you care about yourself sends negative messages.

• Maintain a positive self-image. Others often think you look better than you think you do.

• Think about the good things that have happened to you.

• Listen to your self-talk. If your inner conversation is negative, change it to be positive and constructive.

Positive and negative are but two sides of the same coin only facing different directions.

–Al Schneider

PART III-GENERAL TIPS-BEHAVIORAL

LAUGH

Laughter releases powerful stress-relieving substances (endorphins) into our bodies. It shows others that we are likable and approachable. Laughter is good medicine.

• Help lower communication barriers.

• Release tensions and relax.

• Establish rapport.

• Accept other people's ideas.

• Laugh at yourself. It makes you more likable.

• Avoid laughing at others' mistakes.

....

Laugh and the world laughs with you; Weep, and you weep alone; For the sad old earth must borrow its mirth, but has trouble enough of its own.

–Ella Wheeler Wilcox

PART III–GENERAL TIPS–BEHAVIORAL

USE GOOD MANNERS

Good manners are always appropriate and may give you a competitive edge.

• Say such things as "please, thank you, excuse me" with sincerity.

• Show respect for other people. It improves your communication.

• Pay attention to good manners.

  -They create the right environment for effective communication.

  -They help us to establish rapport.

When someone says, "I'm sorry," it may be an expression of empathy or regret. It does not mean they are taking full responsibility for what happened.

PART III–GENERAL TIPS–BEHAVIORAL

RECOGNIZE MANIPULATIVE BEHAVIOR

To influence without manipulation is an art. To manipulate or control artfully or by shrewd use of influence especially in an unfair or fraudulent way.
(Paraphrasing Webster's definition)

• Be direct.

• Treat others with respect.

• Give convincing arguments. Let others decide for themselves.

• Realize that manipulative behavior can backfire.

PART III–GENERAL TIPS–BEHAVIORAL

RECOGNIZE CONDESCENDING MANNERS

To condescend is to "talk down" to the other person. It is seen as going down to another level, attempting to appear gracious or affable to inferiors.

- Treat others as equals.

- Avoid feeling superior to others. Your verbal and non-verbal language will reflect your attitude.

- Show genuine respect for each individual's uniqueness.

- Avoid prejudging.

A sure way for one to lift himself up is by helping lift someone else.

–Booker T. Washington

PART III–GENERAL TIPS–BEHAVIORAL

AVOID WORDS THAT HURT

A measure of one's stature is consideration for others. But truthfulness can be turned into a hurtful weapon.

- Provide feedback or evaluations only when requested.

- Think of your role in the relationship before providing criticism. Are you teacher, parent, peer, or friend?

- Phrase your criticism to include something positive along with specific suggestions for improvement.

- Don't get personal.

- Allow the other person to save face.

- Avoid embarrassing the other person.

··

I expect to pass through this world but once; any good thing therefore that I can do, or any kindness that I can show to any fellow-creature, let me do it now; let me not defer or neglect it, for I shall not pass this way again.

–Stephen Grellet
Attributed

PART III–GENERAL TIPS–BEHAVIORAL

CHANGE ABRASIVE BEHAVIOR

Some people believe that abrasive behavior causes others to become more submissive. This belief is usually found in superior/subordinate relationships. However, abrasive behavior tends to lead to an abrasive reaction.

• Tone down your verbal and nonverbal abrasive behavior or reactions.

• Show genuine respect for the other person.

• Realize that there are no winners in an abrasive situation.

·······································

Don't confuse being stimulating with being blunt.

–Barbara Walters

PART III-GENERAL TIPS-BEHAVIORAL

HANDLE DISAGREEMENTS WITH TACT

It is unrealistic to think that everyone will always agree with your opinions and go along with what you request. What do you do when the other person says "no?"

• Stay calm.

• Weigh the importance of agreement. If it is a matter of principle, you may decide to end the conversation, or even the relationship.

• Be certain you clearly understand the issue.

• Ask questions until you are satisfied that you have a mutual understanding.

• Accept the response as a difference in opinion, rather than a personal rejection.

• Respect the other person's right to their opinion.

• Work at finding an acceptable compromise unless it is a matter of principle.

••

It is good to rub and polish our brain against that of others.

–M. E. de Montaigne

PART III–GENERAL TIPS–MISCELLANEOUS

ORGANIZE PRODUCTIVE MEETINGS

Whether you are chairing a meeting or participating, consider your purpose and the contribution you will make to the proceedings.

When you are the Chair:

• Prepare. Have a specific purpose for the meeting and an expected outcome.

• Develop a written agenda and have a copy for each participant. It is best to send the agenda to participants in advance.

• Call key participants to ensure they know what is expected of them and have time to prepare.

• Control the meeting by:

   -Sharing and enforcing ground rules.
   -Listening.
   -Allowing free exchange of ideas.
   -Using win-win techniques.
   -Summarizing.

• In formal meetings, arrange for a parliamentarian to serve.

Participants:

• Know your reasons for attending a specific meeting and your expected outcome.

• Stick to the agenda once it's approved.

PART III–GENERAL TIPS–MISCELLANEOUS

CONSIDER THE EXPERIENCE LEVEL OF THE OTHER PERSON(S)

Learn what you can about the person(s) with whom you will be speaking prior to the conversation or meeting. This will enable you to phrase your comments more appropriately.

• Recognize the experience level of the other person.

• Evaluate your listener's experience by asking questions.

• Explain complicated concepts if your listener has less experience than you.

A prudent person profits from personal experience; a wise one from the experience of others.

–Dr. Joseph Collins

PART III–GENERAL TIPS–MISCELLANEOUS

UNDERSTAND THE IMPORTANCE OF TIMING

Just as in any game or sport, timing is very important in conversation.

• Be attuned to the mood of the other person(s).

• When joining a group, listen to get the drift of the conversation before adding your comments.

• Look for appropriate moments to insert your comments.

• Change the conversation tactfully using an appropriate transition.

Observe due measure, for right timing is in all things the most important factor.

—Hesiod

PART III–GENERAL TIPS–MISCELLANEOUS

PRESENT A GOOD PERSONAL IMAGE

People form preliminary opinions about us before we speak a word. Our clothing, grooming, and demeanor send the first signals.

- Use the list below to give yourself a personal image check-up.

- Clean-shaven or neatly trimmed facial hair.

- Fresh make-up.

- Teeth in good repair and recently brushed.

- Hair styled and combed attractively, not radically, unless that's the specific message you intend to send.

- Nails cleaned and trimmed.

- Suit/dress classic or stylish not trendy. Clean, freshly pressed clothing with no loose threads in sight.

- Wear colors suited to the occasion that are becoming to you.

•••

Nothing better reflects our positive attitude than positive appearance. Looking your best is the right approach to being your best.

–Larry Welch

ABOUT THE AUTHORS

JO CONDRILL, GoalMinds CEO, is an internationally known speaker, seminar leader and consultant. She is the author of "Leadership: from Vision to Victory in Six Powerful Steps" (Great Speakers Anthology, Vol. 7). Jo specializes in leadership and team building. She helps individuals and organizations create teams committed to actualizing their dreams. Jo's uniqueness is due, in part, to the fact that she speaks from her own experience. She is the only person ever, in the Washington, D.C. area, to lead a 3,000-person organization (Toastmasters) to a #1 ranking worldwide. She also served on Toastmasters' Board of Directors. Jo provides speeches, seminars, and consultation in communications. Her clients include government agencies, associations, and corporations.

Jo holds a Masters Degree in Public Administration from Central Michigan University. She is also a graduate of the U.S. Army War College .

Photography: Jim Johnson, Washington, DC

BENNIE BOUGH, Ph.D.President, Speaking Dynamics!, Inc., is an internationally known speaker, seminar leader and consultant, and is past president of Toastmasters International. With over 35 years of speaking and training experience, he shares first-hand experiences, specializing in how to give effective presentations whether one-to-one or one-to-a-thousand. Besides United States and Canada, he has trained individuals in communication techniques in China, Vietnam, Laos, Pakistan and Taiwan.

His clients include the United Nations Development Program, the Navy Department, the Environmental Protection Agency and the Science Applications International Corporation. He received his Ph.D. in International Relations from George Washington University.

Photography: Jim Johnson, Orange, CA

A SAMPLING OF SPEECHES, SEMINARS, AND WORKSHOPS

JO CONDRILL PRESENTS..
CREATE A TEAM THAT DREAMS YOUR DREAM
from Vision to Victory in Six Powerful Steps
Enroll can-do teammates and achieve your most outrageous goals!
Overcome obstacles with preemptive options.
Create mutually profitable partnerships.

HOW TO COMMUNICATE SO PEOPLE DON'T JUST HEAR YOUR WORDS...THEY LISTEN!
Give a presentation that gets results.
Read your audience and fine tune accordingly.
Develop a lasting level of confidence.

BENNIE E. BOUGH, Ph.D. PRESENTS...
JOY OF SPEAKING: STICKING TO THE BASICS
Increase your awareness to communicate more effectively;
Determine your level of confidence, your role as a contributor, and
your image as a leader; Improve your chances for promotion;
Control your fear.

COMMUNICATION SKILLS DEVELOPMENT WORKSHOP
Understand fear and how to control it.
Develop greater personal confidence and effective speech delivery.
Learn powerful presentation skills.
Improve nonverbal communication skills.
(videotaping speeches with feedback).

**JO CONDRILL AND BENNIE BOUGH, Ph.D.
(INDIVIDUALLY OR TOGETHER) PRESENT...**

**101 WAYS TO IMPROVE YOUR
COMMUNICATION SKILLS INSTANTLY!**

A fast-paced, highly interactive workshop in which participants put into practice some of the ways contained in the book.

Learn how to:

- Speak clearly and ensure your message is understood.

- Practice powerful listening skills.

- Evaluate behavior that may be keeping you from maximum success.

- Maintain a positive attitude that attracts people.

- Synchronize body language with other communication channels.

••

"You were great, Jo, in concept, in planning, in execution and, most certainly, in first impressions."
>   –James Moonan, Education Coordinator
>   National Association of the Remodeling
>   Industry.

Bennie, *"Your training has had lasting impact...your enthusiasm was contagious, and now I have many staff members who volunteer to speak in public."*
>   –Roy D. Morey, Resident Representative
>   UNDP Hanoi, Vietnam

FOR FURTHER READING

Alessandra, Tony, Ph.D., and O'Connor, Michael J., Ph.D. *The Platinum Rule*. New York: Warner Books, Inc., 1996.

Bolles, Richard Nelson. *What Color Is Your Parachute?* Berkeley, CA: Ten Speed Press, 1995.

Brown, Les. *It's Not Over Until You Win!* New York: Simon and Schuster, 1997.

Brown, Lillian. *Your Public Best*. New York: Newmarket Press, 1989.

Canfield, Jack and Hansen, Mark Victor. *The Aladdin Factor*. New York: Berkley Books, 1995.

Canfield, Jack and Hansen, Mark Victor. *Chicken Soup for the Soul*. Deerfield Beach, FL: Health Communications, Inc., 1993.

Crumlish, Christian. *The Internet for Busy People*. Berkeley, CA: Osborne/McGraw-Hill, 1996

Drummond, Mary-Ellen. *Fearless and Flawless Public Speaking*. San Diego, CA: Pfeiffer & Company, 1993.

Frankl, Viktor E. *Man's Search for Meaning: An Introduction to Logotherapy*. New York: Simon and Schuster, Inc., 1963.

Hemsath, Dave and Yerkes, Leslie. *301 Ways to Have Fun at Work*. San Francisco: Berrett-Koehler, 1997.

Johnson, Edward D. *The Handbook of Good English*, Revised & Updated. New York: Facts On File, 1983.

Joseph, Arthur. *The Sound of the Soul*, Deerfield Beach, FL: Health Communications, 1996.

Lichty, Tom. *The Official America Online for Windows Tour Guide*, 2d Ed. Chapel Hill, NC: Vantana Press, Inc., 1994.

Maragulies, Nancy. *Mapping Inner Space*. Tucson, AZ: Zephyr Press, 1991.

Montalbo, Thomas. *The Power of Eloquence*. Englewood Cliffs, NJ: Prentice-Hall, Inc., 1984.

Morris, Tom, Ph.D. *True Success*. New York: G. P. Putnam's Sons, 1994.

Price, Jonathan. *Put That in Writing*. New York: Viking, 1984.

Province, Charles M. *Patton's One-Minute Messages*. Novato, CA: Presidio Press, 1995.

Slutsky, Jeff and Aun, Michael. *The Toastmasters International Guide to Successful Speaking*. Chicago: Dearborn Financial Publishing, Inc., 1997.

Zey, Michael G., Ph.D. *Winning With People*. New York: Berkley Books, 1990.

INDEX

101 Ways to Improve Your Communication Skills Instantly

REQUEST FOR COMMENTS

Challenges in communication are universal! This book is designed to offer concise "how to" tips to help you over-come those challenges. But you may have other tips that could be helpful for our readers. We welcome your own personal tips, as well as your success stories about how this book has helped you improve your communication skills. If your submission is included in future revisions, we will happily acknowledge your contribution.

Please write to us at the following address:

The Catalyst Group
1 Berghem Mews
Blythe Road
London W14 0HN
Tel: 0171 6037779